C000098015

LOVE IS A

PUG

summersdale

LOVE IS A PUG

An Hachette UK Company
www.hachette.co.uk

Summersdale Publishers Ltd
Part of Octopus Publishing Group Limited
Carmelite House
50 Victoria Embankment
London
EC4Y 0DZ
UK

www.summersdale.com

Printed and bound in Malta

ISBN: 978-1-78685-513-8

Substantial discounts on bulk quantities of Summersdale books are available to corporations, professional associations and other organisations. For details contact general enquiries: telephone: +44 (0) 1243 771107 or email: enquiries@summersdale.com.

No pugs were harmed in the making of this book

♥ INTRODUCTION ♥

With their squashed-up wrinkly faces and little pig-like tails, you could say that pugs are a bit odd-looking… but we prefer 'special'. They're gentle, charming and, above all, silly, and what they lack in size they make up for many times over in personality. Plus, as any pug-lover will know, their loyalty knows no bounds (I mean, it's verging on obsessive). What's not to love? This book is a little way of showing how much we love them in return.

SNUG AS A

♥ PUG ♥

IN A RUG

THE PUG IS LIVING PROOF THAT GOD HAS A SENSE OF HUMOUR.

Margo Kaufman

AND YOU SAY

❤ I'M ❤

WRINKLY?!

DOGS LAUGH, BUT THEY LAUGH WITH THEIR TAILS.

Max Eastman

LIFE IS BETTER WITH

♥ A PUG ♥

(OR TWO)

MY LITTLE DOG —
A HEARTBEAT AT
MY FEET.

Edith Wharton

DID SOMEONE

 SAY

SAUSAGES?

WHOEVER SAID YOU CAN'T BUY HAPPINESS FORGOT LITTLE PUPPIES.

Gene Hill

♥ FEELING ♥

PUGTASTIC

A LIFE WITHOUT A PUG IS POSSIBLE, BUT MEANINGLESS.

Loriot

YEAH, I GUESS I AM

💜 PRETTY 💜

MAJESTIC

BUY A PUP AND
YOUR MONEY WILL BUY
LOVE UNFLINCHING
THAT CANNOT LIE.

Rudyard Kipling

I DIDN'T CHOOSE
THE PUG LIFE — THE
♥ PUG LIFE ♥

CHOSE ME

THERE IS NO PSYCHIATRIST IN THE WORLD LIKE A PUPPY LICKING YOUR FACE.

Bernard Williams

IT'S EXHAUSTING BEING
THIS GOSH-DARNED
♥ CUTE ♥

ALL THE TIME

FROM THE DOG'S POINT
OF VIEW, HIS MASTER IS
AN ELONGATED AND
ABNORMALLY CUNNING DOG.

Mabel Louise Robinson

ALL YOU NEED IS

♥ LOVE... ♥

AND A PUG

NO MATTER HOW LITTLE MONEY AND
HOW FEW POSSESSIONS YOU OWN,
HAVING A DOG MAKES YOU RICH.

Louis Sabin

JUST GIMME

♥ FIVE MORE ♥

MINUTES...

NO ONE APPRECIATES THE VERY SPECIAL GENIUS OF YOUR CONVERSATION AS THE DOG DOES.

Christopher Morley

IT NEVER RAINS

♥ BUT ♥

IT PAWS

I AM I BECAUSE MY LITTLE DOG KNOWS ME.

Gertrude Stein

♥ SHAKE YOUR ♥

PUG-BUTT

DOGS ARE MIRACLES WITH PAWS.

Susan Ariel Rainbow Kennedy

UGLY? NEVER.
♥ ADORABLE? ♥

PUG-SOLUTELY!

THE AVERAGE DOG IS A NICER PERSON THAN THE AVERAGE PERSON.

Andy Rooney

MY HOBBIES INCLUDE BEING AT ONE WITH NATURE AND ❤ FROLICKING ❤

IN THE GRASS

DOGS ARE NOT OUR WHOLE LIFE, BUT THEY MAKE OUR LIVES WHOLE.

Roger Caras

JUST CALL

♥ ME ♥

WONDER PUG

A DOG IS THE ONLY THING ON EARTH THAT LOVES YOU MORE THAN HE LOVES HIMSELF.

Josh Billings

I THOUGHT YOU SAID YOU
WEREN'T COMING
♥ HOME FOR ♥

ANOTHER HOUR...

HISTORIES ARE MORE FULL OF EXAMPLES OF THE FIDELITY OF DOGS THAN OF FRIENDS.

Alexander Pope

YOU TALKIN'

♥ TO ♥

_____

ME?

_____

DOGS FEEL VERY STRONGLY THAT THEY SHOULD ALWAYS GO WITH YOU IN THE CAR, IN CASE THE NEED SHOULD ARISE FOR THEM TO BARK VIOLENTLY AT NOTHING RIGHT IN YOUR EAR.

Dave Barry

KEEP CALM
♥ AND ♥

HUG A PUG

THE DOG WAS CREATED SPECIALLY FOR CHILDREN. HE IS THE GOD OF FROLIC.

Henry Ward Beecher

SUNDAY MORNINGS
♥ IN BED... ♥

PUG-SQUISITE

THE GREAT PLEASURE OF A DOG IS THAT
YOU MAY MAKE A FOOL OF YOURSELF WITH
HIM AND NOT ONLY WILL HE NOT SCOLD YOU,
BUT HE WILL MAKE A FOOL OF HIMSELF TOO.

Samuel Butler

IT'S ALWAYS A

♥ GOOD DAY ♥

TO BE A PUG

TO SIT WITH A DOG ON A HILLSIDE ON A GLORIOUS AFTERNOON IS TO BE BACK IN EDEN, WHERE DOING NOTHING WAS NOT BORING — IT WAS PEACE.

Milan Kundera

WILD

♥ AND ♥

FREE

I'VE SEEN A LOOK IN DOGS' EYES, A QUICKLY VANISHING LOOK OF AMAZED CONTEMPT, AND I AM CONVINCED THAT BASICALLY DOGS THINK HUMANS ARE NUTS.

John Steinbeck

WHAT IF I NEVER
♥ FIND OUT WHO'S ♥

_____

A GOOD BOY?

_____

DOGS ARE THE MAGICIANS OF THE UNIVERSE.

Clarissa Pinkola Estés

ALL ABOARD THE PUGMOBILE.
♥ NEXT STOP: ♥

CUTESVILLE.

EVERYTHING I KNOW, I LEARNED FROM DOGS.

Nora Roberts

If you're interested in finding out
more about our books, find us on Facebook
at **Summersdale Publishers** and follow
us on Twitter at **@Summersdale**.

www.summersdale.com

IMAGE CREDITS